heal.

hana kopernik

ISBN: 978-80-570-3247-2

poems,
and illustrations by:
hana kopernik

edited by:
ivana kopernik

cover art by:
veronica mikulova

I hope in the greatest faith,
for this book to find those who need it.

prologue

May the heavens accompany you,
the tenderness, the purity
Oh, how much we're afraid of the emptiness,
the gift in disguise
May it lead you

heal.

The age of Aquarius,
change in the demeanor of our chemicals as
vapor of love releases in the atmosphere,
I am breathing in, fully

And page after page,
all that is out of date, we are burning, anew
and rewritten anthems, thus, the creation
of a forbidden Eden

- *starseed's dust*

hana kopernik

Flesh and bones, under which hides,
longing for passion and adventure,
maybe a bit of all the world can bring

So shall we push it in, or push it through?

And finally, walk the world in these,
maybe less comfortable shoes
we could have it all if we choose -

the path to a new experience

- *without having to know what it has to offer*

heal.

I undress the ego,
for there simply isn't a reason to hide,
for there simply isn't a reason to run,
for there simply isn't a reason to fear,
for there simply isn’t a reason to compete,
with no one else, other than myself

- other than myself

The inner compass
guides me for a good reason
not many see me, for me, stranger
and if I am to keep going in
the right direction, who, if not I,
will know, what needs my attention?

- *intuition*

heal.

The greatest liar of them all,
pretends to be the force
of our nonstop, in a motion world
and it's winning among
half of the living, paralyzes the souls,
and keeps their potential
shrinking, at least, tend we believe
there's safety within fear,
but oh, fearing is a way of keeping
all under control

- *false evidence appearing real*

If I do not allow my mind
to provide shelter for the dangerous thoughts,
I'm safe

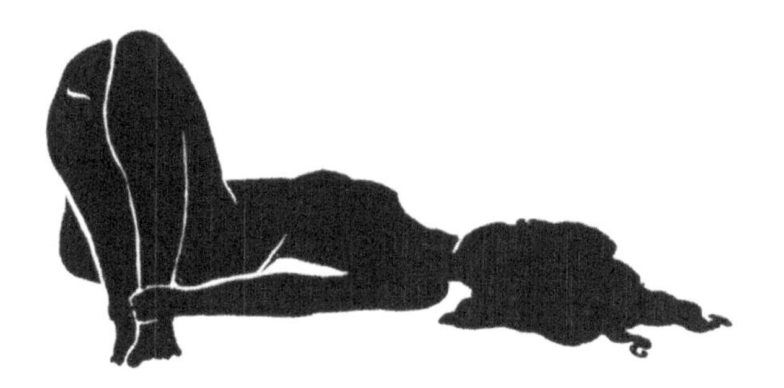

heal.

May we allow
the big shift to come, and heal what we think
can no longer be undone

May we accept
what needs our attention, apologize to one
another and the mother nature

May we tune
into a higher vibration, and work our way
towards a brighter future

- *may we unite*

Offspring of a new millennium,
don't you undervalue the power from within,
the power, flowing through the veins of yours
don't you forget that it is the same exact one
that has created the source

Indigo children, the old souls,
don't you doubt the reason why you came here,
the universe is experiencing itself through the
very eyes of yours, oh, watch the beauty hidden
in its unpredictable tempo

- *111*

heal.

There will come a time
when you'll feel the floor cracking
right under your feet
and you'll no longer be afraid to fall,
for so, it'll no longer
seem as frightening as the first time
you did

- wound healing

The light will guide out
the darkest shadows and the fragments
of a mind that allows safe passage
for the dark

- *shadow work*

heal.

The mind can be a desert, and thoughts its sand
The mind can be the ocean, and thoughts its waves
The mind can be the surface, and thoughts its land
The mind can be a fire, and thoughts its flames

- *do not let it blow, drown, walk over, or burn you away*

hana kopernik

There's no point in wondering what if;

if so,
we could as well,
try counting pieces of dust
on a year-long
forgotten
shelf

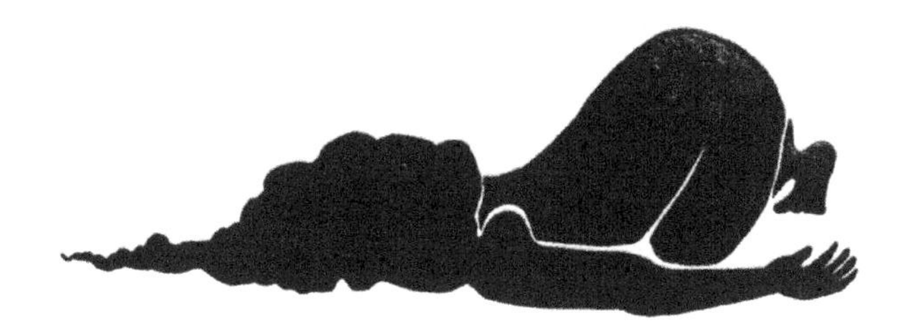

heal.

Sometimes it feels like I fell into a black hole,
but both body and mind got stuck in its membrane
Sometimes it feels like I cannot fill the void,
for its roots reach far beyond what I can reclaim

Event horizon, oh, event horizon

Sometimes it feels like the only way out is when
every inch of hope completely shatters again
Sometimes it feels like it must, to create this life into
a one, that I'd live rather, than any other instead;

Even if the stars collide, oh, even if

- *the suffering will pass*

Don't you settle for the colorless
just because you're too used to the
lack of color

- the midst of a metamorphosis

heal.

I can't keep quiet,
as long as we live along with the all
consuming numbness

I can't keep quiet,
as long as we confuse unconditional love,
with its conditional absence

I can't keep quiet,
as long as we stand and watch as the
theft of souls happens

- I. can't. keep. quiet.

You deserve the kind of love
that will teach you that being you
is enough, to be lovable, too

- *unapologetically*

heal.

healing.
begins by remembering
the person you were before
you were torn
and by letting go of
the reason, that made you believe
that being torn
means no longer being
deserving of
more

hana kopernik

No shift comes,
out of a sudden, to those who suppress
what stops them

heal.

Softness
is a magnificent gift,
to stand against the evil and yet
not become a part of it,
don't you dare mistake such an
act of strength for
weakness

- *divine feminine*

Lioness
don't ever settle for less
when you were made for more,
push to the very edge
of your limits, and from there,
let them hear you
roar

- *divine masculine*

heal.

The paradox is
that you could've done your absolute hardest
fall, right into the darkest of the abyss
and with head held high, begin to climb
without a doubt of stopping
Of course, someone could say that it was
nothing, and someone else could say that they
can’t imagine, but by the end of the day
it wasn’t them, but you, who kept climbing
Take a moment to stop for a while, to be
proud of how you fought your way through
everything, that happened

- take a moment to thank yourself

Time is the greatest luxury
that we have
Though, that does not mean, you have
to be in a rush
before your whole life goes to an end;

- *quite. the. opposite.*

heal.

I felt like a foreigner to human behavior
as a stranger to human nature
If you asked me about it back then, you
wouldn't get the longer answer
I'd feign indifference to the pain, oh if
the walls could talk, they'd say
that behind them nothing but a blame would
occur, I can still vividly see the
fingers pointed in a perfect angle for it
felt like being aimed at by a gun
and although I forgave and I am doing better
I cannot forget the feeling as if
I was the traitor, once I took the courage to
break through the walls and run

- *an escape from a narcissist*

I am not ashamed to be weak
I am not ashamed to be strong
I am not ashamed to be human

- I am only ashamed, of being ashamed, before

heal.

The perpetual pain
lingers, long after midnight hours
and when it rains, it pours,
as I shudder in perpetual
denial

- the curse of remembrance

hana kopernik

I've been told
to settle for those who make me feel
a sense of safety, similar, to the one
I used to feel at home. But what am I
supposed to do, when the only thing
I knew was living in a survival mode,
or what if I have no idea, of how is
a safety or home suppose to feel like?

- *confession past midnight*

heal.

Where did the time go;

after I had to say goodbye to
my childhood and prepare for the worst
sooner than planned

Where did the time go;

after I had to welcome the
dangers that slowly became comfortable
living in my head

- trauma responses

I thought it was over
for the look in my eyes troubled me
as well as the mornings
immersed in sleep for reasons other
than fatigue

- *cyclical suffering*

heal.

Have you already learned to honor the sacred
temple you call the body?

- It holds powers, oh so sacred, that can crush,
even the slightest uncertainty about
the size of yours

Have you already learned to listen to the prayers,
which you call thoughts?

- That speak to you, for you, only you,
in the immortal language, at the forefront
of this mortal life

*- are you still waiting for something bigger
than yourself to come along?*

In solitude,
we are the least alone
for in silence, the soul speaks
and he that heareth,
is he that is whole

heal.

Just like mosaics, parts of us have to break
over and over again, to the point whereupon
they fit together, so utterly,
that suddenly, breaking becomes a blessing

- *who we are we create*

hana kopernik

Once I'll look back at the times
when I had no idea who I was, nor who I should be
at the sleepless nights spend over howling
at the moon, at the lack of iron, at the withered fruit
I'll look back at the last minute decision making
at not knowing what is there for me to do
I'll look back and once it will be damn see-through,
how having nothing left to lose shapes
who we become, how not knowing, to the leap of
faith leads to

- *the leap of faith*

heal.

A feather's in front of my front door,
bumblebees buzz on the porch
as I ask for:

A sign from above

And the clock's been ticking four-four
but a pair of eyes cannot see,
what

A mind cannot grasp

- *non-coincidental coincidence*

Dejavu,
every upcoming moment, just an echo of a bell
Goosebumps, for what I believe
there's a story to tell
And if a sign is to come my way, I am observing
If my heart is to pound, I am listening,
for so the bigger plan reminds itself to us;
everything
that's meant to be is, will be,
and was

- *alignment*

heal.

When you can't see where you're going
in the dark created by dark
When you can't believe in what you're doing
as if blindness shrouded you in
the all-consuming fog,
When you can't tell if you're not standing
there alone, believe me, not at all,
for we are connected one
And who seeks light shall find of it a spark,
for gods' have left the light on
to the seekers that went on the walk

- *keep going, lightworker*

Watch,
as I can dive into
the deepest of the depths,
and on
my way out, unearth
an Atlantis

- piscean

heal.

Only if I could
destroy each beauty standard that goddesses,
like you, cannot be defined by

Only if I could
assure you, that not only man but we as well
age delicately, just like wine

Only if I could
prove that there ain't no expiration date for
the beauty of your kind

- *through my eyes*

Women,
do not forget that we
shouldn't have to prove our worth,
to the society that
would not even be, if no woman
ever gave birth

- *do not forget*

heal.

Dried lavender from Michelle
and the bath is filling, heavy fog spreading
the room, you wouldn't believe the ache
I might be meteo-sensitive but this pain is
way too chronic, it has nothing to do with
an afternoon rain

So cleanse me, sage from Dianne,
I'll light you up in between the thoughts
in which I confess, in which I gasp,
as I wash off yet another day of running
against the clock, against the cycle,
an afterthought

- this cycle, isn't mine

hana kopernik

This is our battlefield
it's us against the mayhem, that wants to see us
kneel but forget that our sisterhood
has fought for way too long, we have lost a lot
of blood, yet they are still disgusted by our menses
Our brothers are resentful,
do not try to make them any more angry,
it's enough that they have to carry this weight on
their shoulders, the fact that you took
their tears and doubled ours, we wept for way too
long for our future sons and daughters,
it's about time to make the 21st century *ours*

- *we need equality*

heal.

Try to look more closely, dreams
are not for dreamers
only

And if hope dies the last, I am sure
it’s because it's dying
slowly

For the universe itself, a product
of the greatest dreamer
may be

And in each of us, there is
the same kind of
holy

hana kopernik

Shake the uncertainty down,
 you are exactly where you're supposed to be
 right here, right now

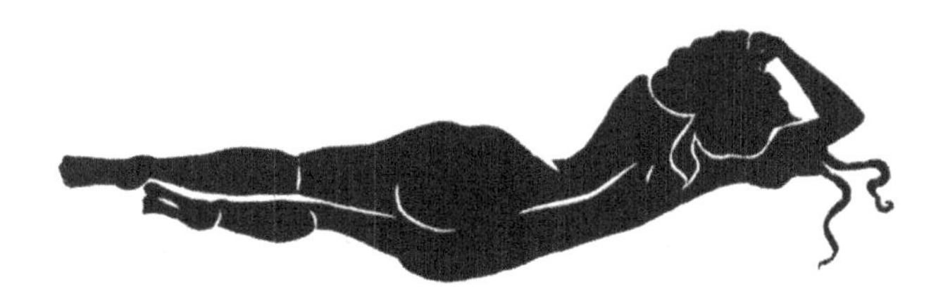

heal.

I want to be somewhere, anywhere but not here
lay under the warm sun whilst the cold breeze
gently eases all of my worries away
I want to be somewhere, anywhere but not here
stand barefoot under waterfalls so giant, their
rage washes off me the weight of the last decade,
therefore, I pray and pray, grab the pen,
trust the time they said, and I shortly got it in a sense;
I want to be somewhere, anywhere but but where,
if not nowhere, would my mind travel on from there?

- *222*

If it's meant to be, it will be
you cannot force a masterpiece,
in the middle of its making

- *universal timing*

heal.

Write your own story,
you are capable to rewrite it anew
yet do not scratch what you cannot undo
Let it sit on the pages,
it's okay if their smell brings out the
old regrets, may the next chapter reveal
why it was crucial to

- *transformation*

The easy way wasn't made for those like you and I,
us, whose ancestors are begging
to be heard until now,
us, who see through things impossible to be
seen by the naked eye
us, who felt too much, too soon, and
whom, was given too little,
we were built precisely, for things
monumental,
for our spirits are capable
to carry much more,
than easy

- *333*

heal.

I am the master of my fate,
guided by the lights, opening the gates
once closed in front of my nose
I'll try to hold them open, countless
of times until I succeed
to get through, and be sure, that I will

- *and if not, I will gladly die trying*

hana kopernik

Dear past,
sharpen my strength for the future to come,
but keep your distance,
I mold and sculpt here and now,
on my own terms

heal.

Fresh ink and Orchids,
I am rewriting and arranging every set
reaction to a memory holding onto me
like a parasite

- self-reflection be my repellent

hana kopernik

I was taught to shine my light in the most
uncertain times when all
living's slumbering, only then, if not ever
I was told that I shine too
bright and that for that, I have no right
when I wasn't destined to be the sun, and I wasn't
I was born to be the moon,
the endless secret, whom everyone should
overlook and diminish,
but be it up to them, I'd be finished

- *scapegoat*

heal.

It sounds like
raw tones of thunder
after an eternity spent in silence
It smells like
a whiff of jasmine,
its vines in a humid climate
It tastes like
a sip of pure water
that has just met pair of dry lips
It's like standing
in front of a mirror, but in its
reflection, stands
a phoenix

- *self-trust*

Let yourself be guided by the heart,
and it will take you places that a sober mind
cannot believe exist

- *444*

heal.

Little did she know,
that once she'll frighten those
who did not believe in her, like a tornado
they rather cover the eyes,
for like a polar light will she glow
Little did she know
that once the feelings, oh
so strong, will erupt, just like a volcano
they rather think twice,
for, from her hard times, she will
make a rainbow after
a rainbow

- *how the phenomena's are made*

A lifetime lesson ahead
one of those that you cannot avoid,
as energy, can only be transformed,
why even would you?

- *self-love*

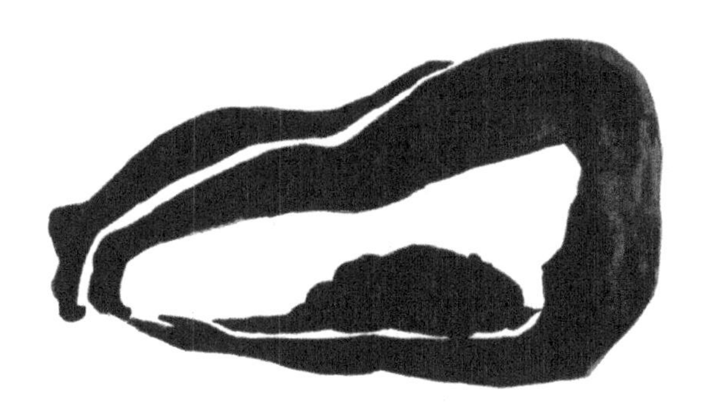

heal.

When I wake up and choose me,
I choose millions of women that came before
and will come, after me
I choose better choices than my mother
had a chance to choose
and that my grandmother, never even could
I choose a voice that my great-grandmother
never had a chance to have,
a voice that gets louder and louder by decades
for my great-granddaughters
to use, whilst they'll one day, take up space

- take up space

Each time
you find comfort
within the inner critic,
you teach the same
the sons and daughters
who'd have a chance to
rebuild the future
on a foundation of love

- *we are the generation to break the bonds*

heal.

Origin of trillions of galaxies,
of different sizes and masses, the Milky way,
its stars, and planets, as well Earth,
upon we walk by, all is made of stardust
It's within me, it's within you

- do not doubt yourself, how even could you?

Unless there's no such place as home
in connection to our own
body

we feel like a cheap apartment in New York -

as if we are taking up space,
made ideally to be
small

heal.

Your potential has existed
since the day you were born

Your life force,
more powerful than one of a hurricane

Your magical energy,
waiting for you to take over

when the time is right, when you are ready

- *you are a blessing*

I am a universal being,
my soul is diametrically different
than my human body

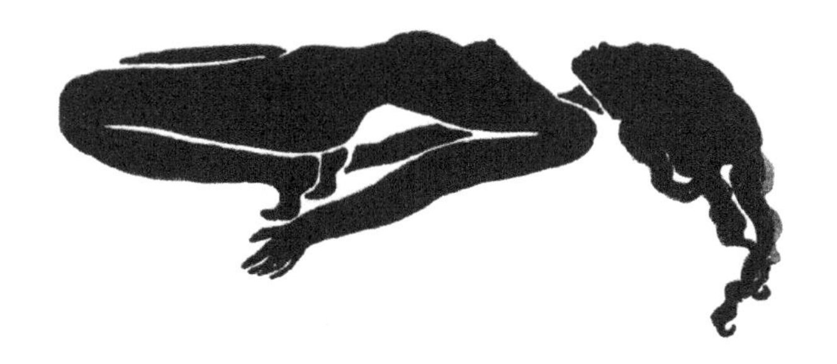

heal.

I want to fully inhabit my body,
and co-create the reality
in a way

my soul rhythm aligns with its nature
that longs to be nothing more,
but free

before anything else, I came here to
become the best version,
of me

- *soul mantra*

Seek silence, the internal kind
in a world where noise, is all around and
external sound compression on a big ratio
Seek silence, hidden beyond
the physical, besides, far beyond logical,
for silence in the midst of a thousand voices
screaming is the epitome of magical

- *the epitome of magical*

heal.

There is no greater intimacy
than the one between you and your naked soul
when you shed layer by layer
of what cannot be grasped in words nor told
cherish it, for there is no purer
of gold

- *inner sanctum*

hana kopernik

You may not see me,
but I glow in the brightest tones
and vibrate in the energy of a warm summer storm.
I am a grounding scent of the gardens, in a valley
underneath the mountain, by the western edge
of Europe

I ain't no ghost,

I am stronger than
the temples, built in times of ancient,
and once in a while I kiss the mirror with red lipstick,
wearing fabric on the skin, but internally
I am naked, elevating the experience
of being

You may not see me,

- *I have to be felt*

heal.

I don't need a “little company"

I'll wait for those who dare to shake me,
like an earthquake
Shake me, abrupt me, move those damn
mountains, that prevent me
from seeing the horizon more clearly
I dare to return the same and much more

- I don't need just a “little company”

hana kopernik

Introduce me,

with the uncomfortable

side of yours,

by the first impression

I'd rather bite

my tongue

a few times now,

than later

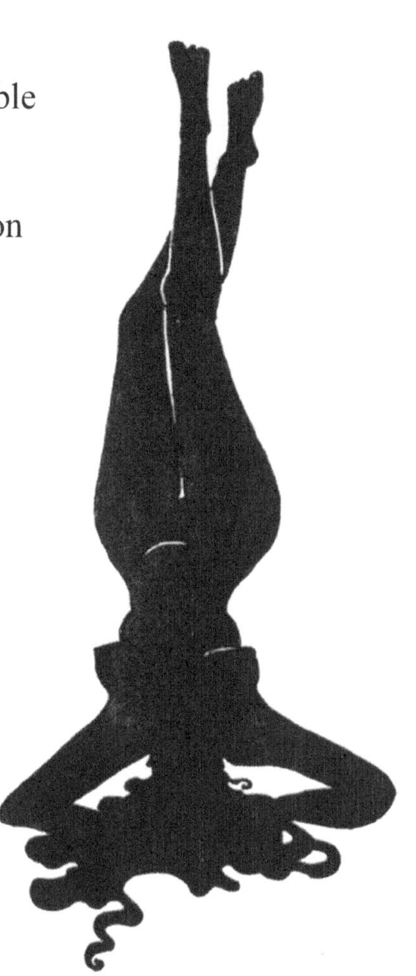

heal.

I used to wish I was born in a different century,
perhaps the naivety spoke for me
A fool who seen hand in hand communities
pulled by the gravity
towards collectively chosen dreams
What I see now when I
look backward, seems the opposite
and what's forward us no one can predict
More than obvious the presence's calling for we
were never meant to be, out of orbit

- 555

We live by patterns we outgrew
The Earth wept, for she saw it happen before,
and knows, what it leads to

- mother nature needs us

heal.

I grew out of waiting for the right time
to come, since I am the only
main instrument needed for the harmony
that I wait for, oh, so damn patiently,
therefore, I'll just play my damn part, and
if it's meant to turn into an
orchestra, the right ones will align

- *solo*

You have what it takes to
turn the wheel of fortune
through a complete devotion
toward the commitment
to be, and to become;
subdue the outcome of the future,
through the state of your mind

- *affirm*

heal.

I am uncovering the dust sheets
thrown over the chambers of my heart
I don't have to wait until the dawn anymore,
I am not afraid anymore,
I am ready to collapse into the light
The power of the unknown within is waking up
like an embryo, a second breath,
and I breathe in, with a yearning for
this life to be fully lived

- 777

hana kopernik

I belong to me, I'm the only thing I have
Even if not at my best
Even if nothing else was left
Even if this material world collapsed

heal.

Is your glass half full
or does every sip of it taste like
the very last?

- fill yourself before you fill others

Woken up by the first rays of the sun,
encircling the walls I practice patience under
And as long as the urge sleeps, and I do not hear
- keep moving forward, you're replaceable -
Oh, you do not own me at all, salamander
keep your little lies to another, who yearns for more
Of course, I do as well, but if I am to live
just to yearn, I won't ever live at all

- the past is gone and the future is far

heal.

I like to lay on the grass in botany gardens
and watch people come and go, in early May
when the morning sky looks as if two
demigods made it, meanwhile making love
and in the evenings, when the sunset
hits slightly different, as I lick off my lips
few ephemeral tears, and a lychee
I am a creature of habit, fueled by emotional
changes, constantly learning to get along
with the presence

- sitting down with my feelings

Once in a while, we have to make a draft
between the head and the heart
and fully breathe in, open both of them wide
To make sure that we either act
out of what we truly need, or out of what
we, undoubtedly, want

- *let it go if it doesn't make you feel alive*

heal.

If I could, I’d do it again
All the joy and delight, all the tears and sorrows
All the *firsts* and *lasts*, even those that
I don't even remember
All of the doubts, decisions, mistakes, the worst
and the most beautiful days
If I could, I’d do it again. For I know that as soon
as I'll get older and reminisce, I will understand
how it all fits together, damn so clearly
all will make sense

- and I am as I am

I let go
of the pressure
to have everything
under control,
for the sake
of my soul's
freedom

- *repeat after me*

heal.

By each year,
I am more further away from the idea of me,
that they made up
upon an unfortunate series of events
Back then,
when I had zero to no muscle
not enough to carry a feather
I learned to levitate,
despite the efforts trying to pull me under,
as a rapid flow of water
set on fire
Able to manage - for now,
and someday
shall be
free

- *dear, it's all temporary*

Why do we put weight onto things?
I'd rather lay under the thunder, naked

- it's less dangerous

When we overthink and
when we don't plan to stop, still

- the future remains unpredictable

When we think the meaning is nearly
within reach meanwhile the entire meaning

- is the meantime

heal.

As a precise crowd psychosis,
the dominoes
fell off

As I promised to withstand,
meanwhile I listen,
to the signs from above

The heart made of stone,
surrendered itself,
to love

- *epiphany*

The manifesto of your life
has been long gone written by the stars

The pathway to your purpose,
drawn, in those imperfect lines on your palms

The answers are flowing from
the ends of your hair, up to their roots

The questions are being answered
the moment you begin to speak your truth

- all you need, you already have

heal.

Wipe the dust under the bed,
before you visualize my silhouette
without wondering whether,
in your idea of me, am I, even interested
When I am trying to be resilient,
against living through the internet, against
the illusion I'd create, you'd misinterpret
When I am trying to be free
of the false identities, made out of the filth,
without the slightest need to
participate, in the judgment of the fallen era
When I stand, without seeking approval,
not to fall

- I am, without seeking approval, to be

I quit with the quick dopamine sensation
if you need me, you'll have to reach me
beyond the notifications

heal.

Promise me, you won't forget
how to laugh as if someone tickled your belly
or climb mountains just as fiercely
and bravely as once you used to climb trees
don't you ever stop wearing cherries
as earrings or eating raspberries off your fingertips
promise me, you won't forget how
to enjoy the little things

- the inner child is ageless

Let me remind you that,
not everyone might see your reflection clearly,
not everyone belongs to the lands you walk on,
the seas you dive into. You, magnificent being

- protect your energy

heal.

When we were young
we pressed shells onto our tiny ears and
believed that through we could hear the
whole entire ocean

When we were young
we said that once, we'll be big, big
enough just as back then our arms at
their length wide open

When we were young
we believed, and others believed in us,
until we tried to reach beyond a horizon
that they had never seen

- projections kill the potential

In front of your success,
stands a failure, ~~impossible~~, for you
to pass

- put the word impossible out of your dictionary

heal.

What would change if you could take a look
into the future, and find out:

the plan for which you sweat blood for,
has worked out
that the places you longed to see,
you walked
that the person you wished for,
came into your life
that the purpose you're searching for,
you've found

- go on, as though it already happened

You are ready to conquer all
of what is yet to come

heal.

If you think you're lost, you are
if you'd like to find a way out, but don't think
there's a way back, there's not

If you think you'll find it, you will
if you'd like to think of the reasons why you can
and not of why not, you win

If you think you can't, you won't
but know, that the moment you dare to think
you can, you have already won

- the power of thought

Life isn't a script
we never know how it turns out
but we can always
take over the director's seat
and be the one
who's in charge of what is, now

- *888*

heal.

To awaken each and every
cell of your body and shake off the thoughts
that fall asleep the mind

To assign meaning
to the important parts of life and leave all that
no longer serves you, behind

To astonish the well-needed
balance between the vision and reality
by being fully aligned

- in the vortex

hana kopernik

It felt like
the fountain runneth over,
secret for secret, I shared, as I drank
though it hasn't waned, not a single drop
It felt like
there wasn't a reason why
should it, for I poured, I poured it up
until the shallow resembled the sky
in aquamarine
It felt like in its reflection,
I've just seen the whole universe shift
though it hasn't changed,
it felt like, it was I,
who did

- *regained hope*

heal.

The soul navigates
as the emotion elevates
surrender
feel the energy in motion
as it pulls you closer to the
wholeness

- *999*

I send blessings upon your healing journey,
dearest reader.

keep in touch

more at:

hanakopernik.com
website

hanakopernik
at instagram

kopernikhana
at twitter

about the author

Hana Kopernik is an author of poetry and prose. She focuses on themes such as self-love, self-growth, activism, and feminism. The aim of her work is to lend a helping hand in a form of her books and words. heal. was inspired by Hana's healing journey and by the transformations that she has gone through within, with the purpose of helping the readers through their very own journey of healing the mind, body, and soul.

The main purpose of heal. is to help the collective regain hope.

I’d love to hear from you

hanakopernik.com/contact

acknowledgments

Thank you, belongs to everyone who helped to make
this -once a dream- of a book, become a reality.
Thank you, to my supporting partner, Peter.
Thank you, to my dearest grandparents, and family.
Thank you, to my greatest team.
Thank you, to my soul sisters Simone, and Rose.
I thank the challengers, teachers, mentors, and
healers that have inspired and transformed me in life.

thank *you*, dearest reader.

Made in the USA
Middletown, DE
31 December 2021

54825816R00064